ASSINIBOINE

HIDATSA

Ft. Union

MANDAN
Ft. Mandan
Ft. Clark
Ft. Lincoln
Ft. Rice
Ft. Yates

Little Missouri River

Red River

HUNKPAPA SIOUX

NORTH DAKOTA

Ft. Abercrombie

Map Legend

N W E S

△△ Native people's territory

Native people's village of earthen mounds

Ρ Wha-shi-choo fort (Ft.)

✕ Battle site

▪▪▪ Wha-shi-choo trail

ARIKARAS

Sitting Bull

MINNESOTA

LAKOTA

CHEYENNE

Cheyenne River

CHIPPEWA

SOUTH DAKOTA

Ft. Pierre

BLACK

HILLS

MINICONJOU SIOUX

PINE RIDGE
INDIAN RESERVATION

OGLALA SIOUX

Missouri River

BATTLE OF
✕ WOUNDED KNEE

IOWA

Ft. Robinson

Niobrara River

GREAT PLAINS

NEBRASKA

North Platte River

ARAPAHO

PAWNEE

Black Elk's Vision
A LAKOTA STORY

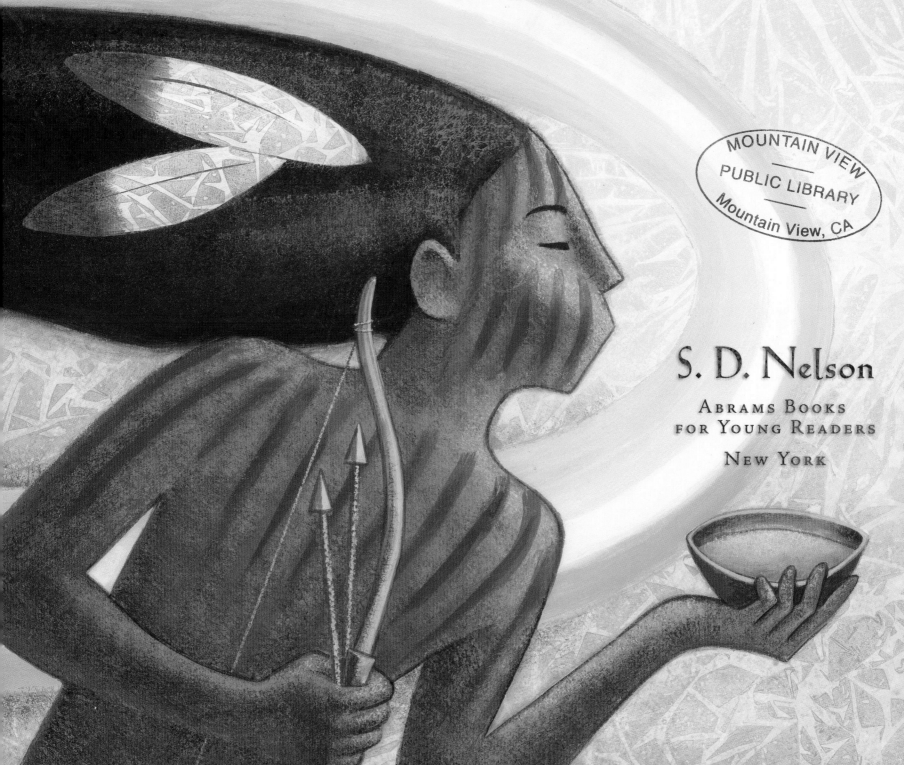

S. D. Nelson

ABRAMS BOOKS
FOR YOUNG READERS

NEW YORK

"...while I stood there I saw more than I can tell and I understood more than I saw; for I was seeing in a sacred manner the shapes of all things..."

—Black Elk

Black Elk with a companion. Elk

Dixon 10º

· 3 ·

"STAY CLOSE TO THE TIPI," OUR MOTHER WARNED.
"If you children wander away, the Wha-shi-choos will snatch you." I had never seen a
Wha-shi-choo. I feared them. They had white faces and had started terrible battles against
our people. So we stayed close to home and played like nervous young rabbits. We knew
enemy eyes could be watching from the tall grass.

I was four years old in 1867 when I first heard the spirit voices. They sounded like my mother calling me. But when I looked she was not there. Then a year later I heard and saw the spirits. I had ridden my pony into the woods near our village. A kingbird chirruped from a tree branch, and the clouds turned dark above. The bird spoke: "The clouds above watch you. A voice calls you. Do you hear?"

A great wind roared in the treetops. Lightning flared all about. Then two Cloud People appeared from the storm overhead. Thunder drummed in my ears, and the two spirits sang:

"Behold, a sacred voice is calling you;
All over the sky a sacred voice is calling."

Rain poured down upon my pony and me. We stood our ground. The spirit of the West Wind whirled all about us. Then the chanting Cloud People turned into geese. Together with the kingbird, the winged-ones flew away into the storm. Although I was only a small boy, I had been shown something extraordinary. I told no one about my vision. I feared they would laugh and call me foolish. Still, I often wondered about what I saw.

Before the Wha-shi-choos came into our country, the Cloud People lived in the blue sky above. There were no wagon roads or iron-horse rails dividing the land. My people, the Lakota, lived freely on the open prairies. We followed the great herds of buffalo. They were our brothers. They provided us with food, and we used their skins to make our clothing and tipis. Along with the women, we children would gather berries and dig for wild turnips from Mother Earth. As I grew older, we boys played at being hunters and warriors. We learned to shoot arrows while riding our horses at a gallop. We wrestled and played many rough-and-tumble games.

ABOVE: Buffalo meat drying near the Yellowstone River. 1877.

RIGHT: Women preparing buffalo hides. Circa 1890.

There were many happy times with good belly laughs. In our village certain men often performed silly antics. We called such men heyokas. They were foolish clowns, and yet they were holy. For laughter itself is a holy gift. Sometimes these men would paint their bodies and wear masks. They usually did things backward—they would say "good-bye" when they meant "hello," or say "I'm not hungry" when they wanted something to eat.

I remember when two heyokas rode on one horse into our village. They rode backward, of course. A crowd of villagers gathered around for the entertainment. One heyoka fell off into a puddle. He splashed around and pretended he was drowning in a great river—which was ridiculous! The other heyoka jumped in to save him. The two men flopped around until they were covered in mud. Finally, they just sat there crying like babies. It was the funniest thing I have ever seen. We all laughed so hard that our stomachs hurt.

The seasons passed—autumn into winter and spring into summer. As I grew older, when I was alone, I would sometimes hear the spirit voices. But I never told anyone. It seemed we had an endless supply of days to be lived beneath the open blue sky. But our world was changing. The Wha-shi-choos, the White People, came into our country looking for the yellow metal they called gold. They made lines on our land with their wagon roads and their iron rails. Still, when the buffalo herds moved, we followed. The Circle of Life held firm against these strange forces.

OPPOSITE AND BOTTOM LEFT: Trains and covered wagons brought more and more Wha-shi-choos west, invading the hunting grounds and territories of the Indians. Circa late nineteenth century.

TOP LEFT: A mining camp sprawls across Lakota hunting grounds in Deadwood, South Dakota. Circa late nineteenth century.

In 1872, when I was nine years old, our entire village was on such a move. Horses carried people and hauled all of our supplies. One day we boys rode our horses beneath a stand of cottonwood trees. Others were laughing and joking, but I felt dizzy and strangely sick. We stopped by a stream to drink and to water our horses. My arms and my legs ached. When I climbed down from my pony, my legs folded beneath me. I spent the night with a fever. The next day I was too sick to ride. Instead, I was laid on a pony drag and pulled all the way to our new encampment. My parents were very worried.

ABOVE: These children peer out from a "cage" that has been lashed to a pony drag much like the one on which Black Elk was carried. The device kept young children from falling off and made traveling easier, as they were too small to ride horses or walk long distances. 1890.

I awoke with a fever, but I still seemed to be sleeping and dreaming. Looking out the doorway of our tipi, I could see the sky. Two spirits came down out of the clouds. These Cloud People called for me to follow. I sat up. My legs did not ache anymore. So I stepped from our tipi into the clouds.

The Cloud People led the way. Mountains of clouds rose all about. Thunder rumbled. Then galloping spirit horses appeared from the four sacred directions. To the west, horses snorted lightning. To the north, they kicked up a snowstorm. From the east, horses pranced with eyes that shone like stars at dawn. And from the south, horses appeared with wind-blown manes growing with grass and the leaves of living trees. They wheeled about me in a great circle.

The plunging horses were in numbers too many to count. Before my eyes they changed into other four-legged beings (deer, coyotes, and rabbits), swimming beings (tadpoles and fish), and winged beings (moths, ravens, and eagles). All of the different animals of the world danced about me in the great Circle of Life.

Suddenly, they vanished into the four directions. I was left standing at the center of the world. A flaming rainbow arced overhead. Before me a tipi appeared. Looking within I saw six old men seated in a circle. "Welcome, grandson," they said. "Enter. Do not be afraid." The faces of the Six Grandfathers looked older than the mountains, older than the stars.

I stepped forward, trembling with fear, for I knew the Six Grandfathers before me were not ordinary old men. They were the ancient ones—the Powers of the World. "Do not fear us, my boy," one spirit reassured. "We have called you here in order to teach you. Share this gift of hope with the Lakota people and all beings living on the good earth."

Another Grandfather handed me a wooden cup filled with water and said, "This is the power to give life that is granted to all." Next he handed me a bow and arrows and said, "This is the power to destroy that is given to all." Everyone must choose to walk with the water of life or the weapon of destruction.

One of the Grandfathers held forth a red stick and said, "This is the tree of life that grows at the center of all things." As he spoke, four leaves sprouted forth. "Carry this sacred stick back to your people. Teach them to care for the tree of life. If all people share the same vision, the tree will flower."

The Six Grandfathers faded into cloud shapes. The shapes became my mother and father, waiting by my bedside. They told me I had lain with a fever for many days. A medicine man from our tribe had prayed over me during that time. He said that I had journeyed to the Spirit World and had been blessed with a Great Vision. I knew he spoke the truth. But I was only nine years old. How was I supposed to share such a powerful vision with my people? So I kept the vision to myself.

After my sickness, people treated me differently. They would come to me when they were sick. They would ask me to pray over them. So I did. Many times they were cured. I often looked up at the clouds and thought about my vision of the flowering tree. I doubted the good words of the Six Grandfathers. I doubted myself, for our way of life was being destroyed around us, and what could my vision do?

The United States government knew we could not survive without the buffalo. So they slaughtered most of them. Then they demanded that the Lakota people sign a paper called a "treaty." That paper took most of our land and forced us to move onto Indian reservations. Soldiers came and fought all Indians who resisted. Many terrible battles followed.

ABOVE: Approximately 40,000 buffalo hides piled up in Rath and Wright's Buffalo Hide Yard in Dodge City, Kansas. They would be shipped east to be made into carriage robes and household rugs. Before the Wha-shi-choo arrived, buffalo numbered an estimated thirty million across the Americas. Unregulated shooting, however, culminating in mass slaughters during the 1870s, reduced the population to about 1,000 by 1889. 1878.

ABOVE: Dead buffalo lying in the snow, killed by Wha-shi-choo hide hunters. 1872.

I remember the hot summer day in 1876 when Lieutenant Colonel Custer, or Yellow Hair as we called him, attacked our village. I was twelve years old. We were camped along the Little Bighorn River where Chief Sitting Bull had called for a council of the Lakota and Cheyenne nations. It was the greatest gathering of Indians that I had ever seen. We numbered in the thousands!

In the heat of midday, we boys were cooling off in the river. Many families rested near their tipis in the shade of cottonwoods. On a hillside I could see women and girls digging for turnips. From the far end of our encampment, we heard a commotion and the cries, "Wha-shi-choo soldiers are attacking!" Bullets cut through the leaves overhead. The ground rumbled from the galloping of charging horses. Without warning, Wha-shi-choo soldiers, or blue coats as we called them, set upon us like a cruel blowing wind. Women and children screamed, running every which way. Crazy Horse, one of our great chiefs, rode forward rallying the warriors. He called out, "Ho–ka hey! It is a good day to fight! It is a good day to die! Strong hearts, brave hearts, to the front!" In the confusion, I grabbed my weapons and mounted a horse.

TOP: George Armstrong Custer, circa 1860–65. At the time this photograph was taken, Custer held the rank of major general of volunteers. After the Civil War, he was appointed to the regular army rank of lieutenant colonel.

BOTTOM: Chief Sitting Bull of the Hunkpapa-Lakota. Circa 1881.

Hundreds of blue coats were attacking. They had come to kill my parents, my brothers and sisters, and my friends and my neighbors. Still, there were thousands of us, and we were fighting for our lives! We had the power as well. Everywhere there were screaming horses and dying people. The gunfire roared like a hailstorm. The furious fighting stirred a dark cloud of dust that smudged out the sun.

Before me in the dim light, I saw a blue coat who had fallen from his horse. I shot him with my pistol, and then I took his scalp. I killed a second soldier with an arrow and later scalped another dead man. Panicked horses ran past me trying to escape from the cloud of death. Their saddles were empty now. In time, the hail of bullets quieted. The dust cloud settled, covering all the slain men and fallen horses. The smell of so much blood gave me a sick feeling. I had to lead my pony away from that awful place.

As for Yellow Hair, he was foolish and died on that terrible day. Most of his soldiers died with him. Although my people won the Battle of the Little Bighorn, as it came to be called, there was little time for celebration. We gathered up our belongings and fled toward the west. We knew more blue coats would come. And they did, in numbers no one could count, to hunt us. We were helpless against so many guns. Chief Crazy Horse led us as best he could. With no buffalo to hunt, we were hungry. In the cold of winter, we began to starve. When our horses died, we ate them. There was nowhere else to turn. My defeated people gave up their guns. We surrendered our way of life.

RIGHT: A picture of dead Wha-shi-choo soldiers at the Battle of the Little Bighorn, drawn by Lakota chief Red Horse. 1881.

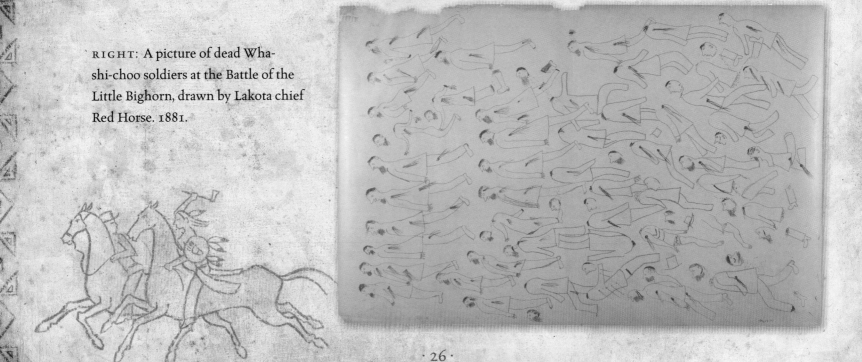

ABOVE: Black Elk's people camped near Fort Robinson (where Crazy Horse was killed) and would have looked similar to this forced encampment of Sioux within a fenced enclosure on the Minnesota River. Circa mid- to late nineteenth century.

We camped near the soldiers' fort on the land now called an Indian reservation. Even though Chief Crazy Horse had come willingly and brought his people to the Wha-shi-choos, the soldiers tried to imprison him. Crazy Horse struggled with them, and they killed him. I was heartbroken and cried the whole night through. The power of life I had seen in my vision seemed to be broken. I lost all hope for a flowering tree of goodness.

We no longer hunted to support ourselves. Instead, the government gave us food and blankets. Our entire way of life had been turned on its head. My people felt like a wounded animal—we were pinned in a cruel steel trap with no hope of escape. I was sixteen years of age. Sometimes I would awake before dawn, when the Morning Star still shone in the sky. I would crawl from our tipi while everyone in our village slept. Standing alone in the stillness, I would hear the spirit voices whispering. They scared me. I did not know what they wanted of me.

Whenever storm clouds appeared, I would tremble, for the Thunder Beings chanted to me, "Behold your Grandfathers! Make haste." In the daytime birds would often call to me, and at night coyotes would howl, "It is time. It is time."

Finally, an old medicine man named Black Road offered me hope. I told him about the troubling voices and my Great Vision. He listened carefully, then told me, "My boy, you have been blessed with a holy vision. The spirit voices are telling you that it is time to share your vision with the people of this world." Black Road told me I needed to perform a Horse Dance ceremony for our entire tribe.

Black Road and a man named Bear Sings set up a ceremonial tipi. Upon it they painted the images of my wondrous vision. Over the doorway arched the colors of a flaming rainbow. Seated inside, I was joined by six old men, just like the Six Grandfathers who are the Powers of the World. They told me I had become a teacher and a healer. Outside, the Thunder Beings rumbled their approval. People gathered, leading horses that they had painted in a sacred manner. They brought a painted horse especially for me.

The Grandfathers sat with a cup of water and a bow with arrows. They said, "Be brave and go forth." So I passed through the doorway of the flaming rainbow and mounted my pony. A throng of people mounted on dancing horses circled the tipi. Everyone celebrated my vision in the clouds. All the people of my village sang to the rhythm of beating drums and the thunder above. Courage filled my heart as they gathered, listening for my words. I told them about the cup of water and the bow and arrows. I explained that every person carries the power to give life and the power to destroy. With the strength of my vision, I called out my message of hope—"Each of you is like a blossom that flowers upon the Tree of Life. Grow strong. Let your branches fill with budding leaves and singing birds."

By performing the Horse Dance ceremony, I had shared the knowledge of my Great Vision. All fears and doubts about my vision were washed away. Still, there seemed to be no future for my people living on the Indian reservation. The buffalo were gone. We could not move. The Circle of Life was broken.

In 1886 a Wha-shi-choo showman named Buffalo Bill Cody offered us a job performing in his Wild West show. The great Lakota chief Sitting Bull joined his show. So did other Indians. I thought about my vision—maybe, if I joined with the others, I might learn more about the strange and powerful world of the White People. If I went among the Wha-shi-choos, maybe I would overcome any weakness still inside of me. With renewed strength I could help mend the broken circle of my people.

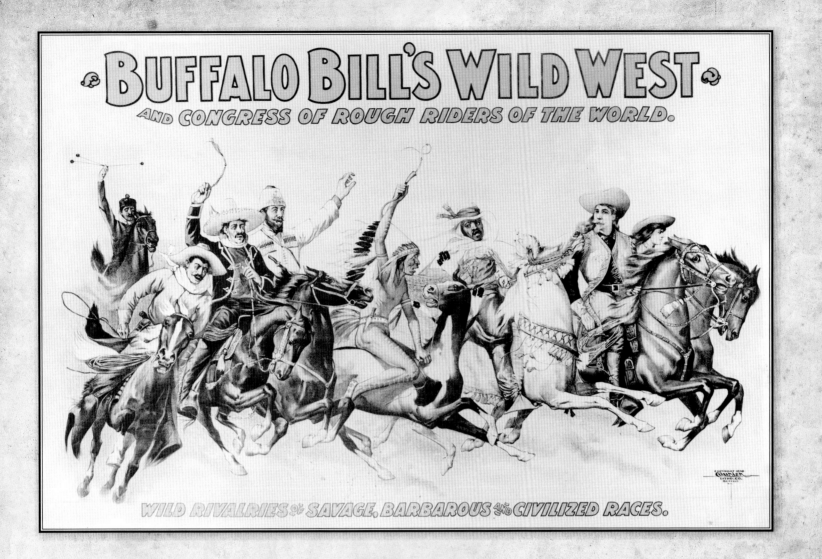

We rode an iron horse far away to the city of New York. The power of the Wha-shi-choos was greater than I had ever imagined! They lived in tall stone buildings that glowed with light in the night. Crowds of people paid money to see us Indians in a big outdoor circus. We rode horses and pretended to hunt buffalo. We wore our native clothing, sang our songs, and played at fighting soldiers. At the end of every performance, we Indians would pretend to be killed. Buffalo Bill would ride into the big arena on his great white horse. He shot his pistol with no bullets, and we Indians fell down like we were all dead. The crowds of people cheered to see the great spectacle.

RIGHT: Portrait of eight Native American men wearing traditional regalia and William F. Cody in western attire holding rifle. Left to right: (Pawnee) Brave Chief, Eagle Chief, Knife Chief, Young Chief, Buffalo Bill, (Sioux) American Horse, Rocky Bear, Flies Above, Long Wolf. Circa 1886.

It seemed strange that people who put us on reservations also admired us. The Wild West show was a great success. Buffalo Bill took the show across the big-water to Europe. All of the members of the show, including the horses and buffalo, were gathered on a huge fireboat. We journeyed many days upon the big-water. While at sea a terrible storm set upon us. The ship rolled up and down on mountains of water. Many Indians vomited with sickness. At first the sailors laughed. Then terror filled their eyes, too. They also feared the great fireboat would be swallowed. They told us to put on vests that would float on the big-water. I refused. Instead, I dressed myself in the manner of a Lakota warrior. I beat my drum and sang prayers to Wakan Tanka, the Great Spirit who is the one power in this world.

The storm passed. Some of the animals had died upon the ship. It broke my heart to see the bodies of elk and buffalo thrown overboard. Just the same, we had crossed the great ocean. Thousands of people came to see our Wild West show in London. Buffalo Bill paid all of us, and he treated us fairly. But I always thought about my family and my vision of the sacred tree. I often wondered how I was supposed to continue sharing the teachings of the Six Grandfathers.

ABOVE: Members of Buffalo Bill's Wild West show aboard the steamship *State of Nebraska* bound from New York to England. Circa 1887.

ABOVE: The Ghost Dance ceremony was performed to bring back the slaughtered buffalo and slain family members. Date unknown.

While in England, I joined another Wild West troupe, the Mexican Joe show. We performed in France, Germany, and Italy. In 1889 I returned to my family on the Pine Ridge Indian Reservation. I had been away for nearly three years and was twenty-six years old. I was so happy to be home again and to see my parents. But life on the reservation was worse than when I left. There was never enough food. In the winter, without enough warm clothing or shelter, my people suffered, and many died.

In the cruel winter of 1890, the Lakota people had become desperate. We longed for the old days when we hunted buffalo and lived freely on our Mother Earth. Many gathered to pray in secrecy on the prairie. In a circle we danced the Ghost Dance. We prayed for the buffalo to return. I believed the vision of my youth would come true. I hoped a miracle would cause the Tree of Life to flower for my people. But the blue coats hunted us, and many of my Lakota people retreated to a place called Wounded Knee.

Wha-shi-choo soldiers gathered on the hilltops surrounding the village of tipis at Wounded Knee. In their hearts they carried the power to destroy. The battle and skirmishes that followed would be the last fight of my people. More than three hundred Lakota men, women, and children were gunned down in the snow at Wounded Knee. I was shot in the stomach but lived to tell my story. At the time, I thought the Circle of Life of my people had been broken forever. It seemed the Tree of Life had been crushed to death in the snow.

ABOVE: Members of Battery E of the 1st Artillery pose with Hotchkiss guns used against the people at Wounded Knee. 1891.

LEFT: U.S. soldiers put Indians in a common grave after the Battle of Wounded Knee. Some of the corpses are frozen. 1891.

RIGHT: After the Battle of Wounded Knee, a group of children, an elderly man, and some women pose for a moment outside their tipis. 1891.

My people and I surrendered to the Wha-shi-choos. We moved onto the Pine Ridge Reservation. We were not allowed to roam the plains any longer.

The road I have walked in this life has been both wonderful and hard. I am an old man now. But I remember the endless supply of days lived by a boy riding his pony beneath a blue sky. In my memory, I can see the terrible suffering of my people. I ask, Why have human beings forgotten that the earth is their mother? But I am not bitter. I still walk with the Great Vision in my heart. Like the Six Grandfathers, I now give you the same gifts they gave me. To you I pass the bow and arrows, with the power to destroy. Also, I pass you the cup of water, with the power to give life.

I ask, Where is the flowering tree I saw as a boy . . . ?

If you look with your heart, you will see the thirsty little tree
before you. In your hands is the power to help it grow.

NICK BLACK ELK AND FAMILY
CATHOLIC CATECHIST.

Author's Note

Understanding the Great Vision

A vision comes as a thunderstorm in summer. Its gift is like rain upon a thirsty little tree.
—S.D.N.

AS YOUNG BLACK ELK LAY WITH FEVER, BETWEEN WAKING AND dreaming, the Great Vision came to him. The boy had not sought a vision; instead, he had been summoned into the Spirit World.

His profound experience is uniquely Native American, filled with images of painted horses, rabbits, deer, and rumbling Thunder Beings. Yet what he witnesses speaks to something fundamental in the human experience—the universal quest to connect with the all-encompassing force that is the Great Mystery. For it is the desire of all people in all cultures to find our purpose in this life. Black Elk's journey takes him beyond the clouds to the center of creation. He enters the realm of spirits, where a flaming rainbow arcs overhead and the stars forever burn.

The boy is welcomed into the lodge of the Six Grandfathers. These mythic ancestral figures possess eternal wisdom. They show Black Elk that we two-legged beings dance in the Circle of Life with all of our brothers—the four-legged, the winged-ones, the green-growing beings, and even the little creepy-crawlies. All beings are to be respected, for all have souls. In truth, we depend on all of the creatures in this world. For in order to survive, we humans must consume plants and animals—life must be taken so that we may live. It is only with this awareness that we learn humility and find balance. Our lives need to be lived in a circle, not in a square, nor a straight line.

For Native Americans the Circle of Life is real. If you look, you will see—the sun and moon are round, circling above us. The earth that turns beneath our feet is also round. The changing seasons come and go in a circle. All of life is one great circle made up of many little circles—like a bird's nest, woven to encircle its clutch of little round eggs. We are born from

OPPOSITE: Black Elk with his wife and daughter. Circa 1900.

the womb of Mother Earth. We dance our entire life in a circle—as crawling babies and then as walking children with curious eyes. We become adults who shape the world for better or worse, then elders who share the wisdom. We continue in the circle by returning to Wakan Tanka, the Great Mystery. Our spirits join the Star People who dance along the White Road of the Milky Way galaxy, which turns round in a great spiral of stars.

Black Elk dreamed his Great Vision of hope against a changing landscape of horrible destruction. Throughout human history there has been bloody conflict between different cultures. Some groups of people stubbornly insist they are better than others and are "above" them. Black Elk hoped that his teachings would contribute to our common good. He wanted human beings to change how they "see" and find *connection* to the world around us. We can no longer rule over the beasts of the earth and seek "dominion" over our environment. We human beings are not privileged beings who are above or separate from the world. We are *part* of the landscape and everything in it. With this awareness comes humility and the gift of harmony.

About This Book

The Lakota word for white man is "Wasichu." (I have chosen to hyphenate the word in order to clarify its three-syllable pronunciation—Wha-shi-choo.) The Wha-shi-choo, or Euro-Americans, advanced upon the continent to take gold, timber, the vast supply of animal furs, and the land itself. Their conquest of the Native Americans was absolutely stunning. They possessed advanced technologies, written language, political organization, and immunity to Old World diseases. In what is now called the "Clash of Cultures," the Wha-shi-choo literally railroaded, or over ran, the Native American culture. Driven by industrial might and an arrogant belief in "Manifest Destiny"—the white man's right to take whatever he desired—they *took* everything in their path. In the process they slaughtered an estimated thirty million buffalo, driving the species to near extinction; fewer than one thousand survived. They steamboated up the rivers, built forts, and waged war with their cannons. In a most frightening manner, they unintentionally brought diseases to which the Indians possessed no immunity. Hundreds of thousands of Native Americans died from measles, smallpox, and influenza. It was common for 80 to 90 percent of entire villages to perish during such epidemics.

Originally, the Lakota, also called the Sioux, had lived in the woodlands of Minnesota, where they cultivated gardens of corn, beans, and squash. They were hunters and gatherers, all of which they did on foot. In the mid-1700s the Chippewa, who had acquired guns from English and French traders, forced the Lakota from the region. At the same time, the horse was introduced onto the Great Plains from the south. The Lakota adapted to their new situation immediately. They gave up farming, learned to ride horses, and acquired guns. Once mobilized on horses, they became a feared nomadic warrior society. They formed alliances with certain tribes, including the Cheyenne. However, they constantly fought for territorial domination with other tribes, such as the Crow and Arikara. The Lakota were greatly respected for their skills in warfare. Nonetheless the Wha-shi-choos proved to be even more aggressive and expansionist than the Lakota. The Stone Age tools and weapons of the Indians—spears, clubs, bows and arrows—were no match for the massive firepower, diseases, and industrial might of the Wha-shi-choos. By the late 1800s the Lakota were beaten. They submitted and moved onto tracts of land called reservations, where they remain to this day.

Black Elk and his Oglala-Lakota band accepted their assignment and settled on the Pine Ridge Indian Reservation in South Dakota. Eventually, he married and raised a family. He even embraced Christianity, for he believed its teachings of acceptance and understanding were compatible with the Indian Way. In 1930 an author named John Neihardt sought out Black Elk. The old medicine man agreed to tell his life story, resulting in the inspirational book *Black Elk Speaks*, published in 1932.

Among his people Black Elk was a respected holy man. He lived to be eighty-seven years old and is buried upon the Dakota prairie he loved. In his youth, surrounded by overwhelming destruction, he saw beyond the pain and dreamed a beautiful vision. Among the many lessons found in Black Elk's vision is this: All human beings have the *power of choice*. Through our actions we choose either to destroy life or to give life. It is no good to live our days with a blaming heart; that way leads only to suffering. We are not victims of a destiny forced upon us by others. Instead, we are the makers of our people's future. If we truly seek harmony, we will choose to carry the wooden cup of water. It alone holds the power to give life.

• • •

Select Timeline

- **1541**—The Spanish conquistador Coronado explores present-day Kansas on horseback. Leading his expedition from Mexico, he is the first European to encounter American Indians on the southern Great Plains. It is also the first time Plains Indians have ever seen a horse. Thereafter, the horse becomes a prized trade item among the Native Americans and a vehicle that will change their way of life.

- **1680**—The first horses are acquired by the Lakota Sioux of the northern Great Plains.

- **1691–1700s**—French, British, and Spanish fur traders are the first white men to make contact with the Native American inhabitants of the northern Great Plains. In exchange for animal furs, Indians receive glass beads, guns, metal implements, and cloth. Diseases, including smallpox and measles, are unintentionally passed to Indians with devastating results.

- **1764**—The Pennsylvania colony offers 134 pieces of eight "for the scalp of every male Indian enemy above the age of ten."

- **1769**—A Spanish mission is founded in present-day San Diego, California.

- **1778**—The first treaty between the U.S. government and Native Americans is made with the Delaware Tribe. The contract is broken and rewritten eighteen times during the following century. Eventually, the Delawares are forced onto an Indian reservation in Oklahoma.

- **1781**—The Mandan, Hidatsa, and Shoshoni tribes are devastated by smallpox.

- **1803**—The Louisiana Purchase. The U.S. government buys the vast expanse of land roughly from the Mississippi River to the Rocky Mountains. The countries of Spain and then France had previously claimed the tract of land from the Indians.

- **1804**—Lewis and Clark lead the Corps of Discovery into the land newly acquired through the Louisiana Purchase, where they meet eleven of the tribes inhabiting the area.

- **1829**—President Andrew Jackson calls on Congress to move Indians living in the Southern states to a reservation in present-day Oklahoma. So begins a ten-year roundup and eventual relocation of sixty thousand Indians. More than two thousand Cherokee die on the long, cruel march called the Trail of Tears.

- **1832**—The first steamboat travels up the Missouri River into the land of the Lakota Sioux. Many steamboats follow, creating an explosion in river travel and a boom in fur trading.

- **1834**—A fur-trading outpost, which will be called Fort Laramie, is established on the North Platte River in Wyoming. It becomes the major stopping place for fur traders, missionaries, Indian trappers, and emigrants.

- **1837**—A smallpox epidemic almost exterminates the Mandan tribe.

- **1848**—Gold is discovered in California. In search of riches, tens of thousands of emigrants begin crossing Indian Territory.

- **1851**—The great treaty council is held between the U.S. government and the many tribes of the Great Plains. An agreement is struck for Indians to allow thousands of emigrants to pass unharmed through their lands. In exchange, the Indian tribes will receive food, clothing, and other goods for the next fifty years.

- **August 19, 1854**—The Grattan Battle. The U.S. government does not provide the food and goods promised in the 1851 treaty. Hungry Indians steal and kill a cow from an emigrant wagon train. A confrontation occurs in which thirty soldiers are killed. In the same year, the army counters with an attack on a Lakota village at Blue Water Creek. Eighty-six men, women, and children are killed.

- **1861–1865**—The Civil War between the Northern and Southern states moves the U.S. military's focus away from the conflict with the Indians.

- **1861**—The Dakota Territory is formed by the U.S. Congress for settlement.

- **1862**—The Homestead Act gives settlers vast areas of land previously occupied by Indians.

- **December 1863**—**Black Elk** is born near the Little Powder River in the Montana Territory.

- **November 29, 1864**—The Sand Creek Battle. At dawn seven hundred military volunteers attack Chief Black Kettle's encampment, killing more than one hundred Cheyenne men, women, and children. They return to Denver, Colorado, with scores of Indian scalps.

- **1865**—The Harney-Sanborn Treaty is signed between the U.S. government and the Indians. The vast Powder River Region is given to the Native Americans. Nonetheless, gold had been discovered in Montana in 1862, and thousands of emigrants seeking wealth flood into the area.

- **December 27, 1866**—The Fetterman Battle. Eighty-one U.S. soldiers are killed in a battle with Crazy Horse and a force of Lakota, Cheyenne, and Arapaho warriors. Black Elk's father suffers a serious leg injury in the fight.

- **1868**—The railroad reaches the Dakota Territory.

  The Battle of the Washita—Lieutenant Colonel George Armstrong Custer leads a U.S. Army attack against a sleeping Cheyenne village. More than one hundred men, women, and children are killed. Indian horses numbering eight hundred are rounded up and shot. The Indians now have no means of transportation or escape.

  The Treaty of Fort Laramie reaffirms the Harney-Sanborn Treaty of 1865, which gives the Black Hills to the Native Americans. Five-year-old Black Elk has his first vision.

- **May 10, 1869**—The First Transcontinental Railroad is completed. The link between the east and west coasts of the country is complete. Ultimately numbering in the millions, the influx of emigrants will be unprecedented and overwhelming.

- **1872**—Black Elk is nine years old when he has his Great Vision.

- **1874**—The Black Hills Expedition. Custer leads an army of one thousand men into the Black Hills, where they discover gold. Within a year, thousands of miners enter the area in search of the precious metal. This violates the Treaty of Fort Laramie. Indian warriors respond by randomly attacking the white intruders.

- **1875**—General Philip Sheridan states that by exterminating all of the remaining buffalo herds, the Indians would be deprived of their primary food source: "For the sake of lasting peace, let them [hunters] kill, skin, and sell until the buffaloes are exterminated." It is estimated that, within twenty years, fewer than one thousand buffalo remain in North America. Originally, there had been an estimated thirty million buffalo on the Great Plains.

- **May 1876**—A military force of thousands of cavalry and infantry converges on the Powder River region to subdue the Indians and force them onto smaller areas of land called Indian reservations.

- **June 25, 1876**—The Battle of the Little Bighorn in the Montana Territory. Custer and the 7th Cavalry attack the Lakota Sioux and Cheyenne encampment in the Montana Territory. It is possibly the largest encampment of Indians ever assembled on the Great Plains. There are hundreds of tipis, with approximately eight thousand people (two thousand are warriors). Black Elk, twelve years old, is involved in the fight for his people, and he cuts the scalps from two fallen cavalrymen. Custer and 262 of his men are killed.

- **1877**—Thousands of U.S. soldiers are massed against the Indians of the Plains. The Lakota chief Sitting Bull and his Hunkpapa band retreat to safety in Canada.

  Congress illegally reclaims the Black Hills from the Indians.

- **May 6, 1877**—The Lakota chief Crazy Horse and his starving Oglala band surrender to the U.S. Army at Fort Robinson, Nebraska.

- **September 6, 1877**—During negotiations with the commander of Fort Robinson, Crazy Horse is threatened with arrest and imprisonment. He resists and is bayoneted by soldiers. The Lakota chief dies in the early hours of the next morning.

- **1881**—Black Elk performs the Horse Dance ceremony for his entire village.

- **1886–1889**—Black Elk joins Buffalo Bill's Wild West show. They perform in New York City and then travel to England. Black Elk then tours Europe with the Mexican Joe show.

- **1889**—South Dakota declares statehood.

- **1890**—More than 328,000 European Americans have settled in South Dakota on land that had been Indian country.

- **December 15, 1890**—Sitting Bull is assassinated on the Standing Rock Indian Reservation.

- **December 29, 1890**—The Battle of Wounded Knee, also referred to as the Massacre at Wounded Knee. In the middle of winter, the U.S. Army attacks a Lakota village in South Dakota. The Lakota suffer a horrible loss: 340 men, women, and children are killed, and this is the last battle of the Indian Wars. Afterward, the defeated Native American people surrender. With the buffalo gone and the Indians near starvation, the tribes move onto the Indian reservations. Native Americans become dependent on the U.S. government for rations.

- **1892**—Black Elk marries for the first time and starts a family on the Pine Ridge Indian Reservation in South Dakota. Together they have three children. (He remarries in 1905 after the death of his first wife. He and his second wife have three more children.)

- **August 1930**—Writer John Neihardt meets Black Elk. The old medicine man agrees to narrate his life's events as a boy and a young man.

- **1932**—*Black Elk Speaks*, by John Neihardt, is published.

- **August 19, 1950**—Black Elk dies on the Pine Ridge Indian Reservation.

Notes

Page 2: "...while I stood there...the shapes of all things..." Quoted in *Black Elk Speaks*, page 43.

Page 7: "The clouds above watch you...Do you hear?" Adapted from *Black Elk Speaks*, page 19.

Page 7: "Behold, a sacred voice...is calling." Quoted in *Black Elk Speaks*, page 19.

Page 18: The faces of the Six Grandfathers...older than the stars. Adapted from *Black Elk Speaks*, page 29.

Page 19: I stepped forward...living on the good earth. Adapted from *Black Elk Speaks*, page 19.

Page 21: "This is the power to give life that is granted to all" and "This is the power to destroy that is given to all." Adapted from *Black Elk Speaks*, page 26.

Page 24: "Ho-ka hey!...to the front!" Quoted in *Crazy Horse and Custer*, page 440.

Page 29: "Behold your grandfathers! Make haste" and "It is time. It is time." Quoted in *Black Elk Speaks*, page 159.

Page 29: "My boy...of this world." Adapted from *Black Elk Speaks*, page 161.

Page 44: "for the scalp...age of ten." Quoted in *The World of the American Indian*, p. 337.

Page 45: "for the sake...buffaloes are exterminated." Quoted in *The Buffalo Hunters*, p. 41.

Bibliography

Ambrose, Stephen E. *Crazy Horse and Custer*. New York: Doubleday, 1975.

Ambrose, Stephen E., and Sam Abell. *Lewis & Clark: Voyage of Discovery*. Washington, D.C.: National Geographic Society, 1998.

Benson, Vera. *Hammond Atlas of the World*. New York: Hammond World Atlas Corporation, 2003.

Berlo, Janet Catherine. *Plains Indian Drawings 1865–1935*. New York: Harry N. Abrams, Inc., 1996.

Billard, Jules B., ed. *The World of the American Indian*. Washington, D.C.: National Geographic Society, 1974.

Buffalo Hunters, The. New York: Time-Life Books, 1993.

Capps, Benjamin. *The Indians*. New York: Time-Life Books, 1973.

Colton, G. W. *Dakota and Wyoming* (archival map). New York: G. W. and C. B. Colton & Company, 1868.

DeMallie, Raymond J. *The Sixth Grandfather*. Lincoln, NE: University of Nebraska Press, 1984.

Diamond, Jared. *Guns, Germs, and Steel*. New York: W. W. Norton & Company, Inc., 1997.

Ewers, John C. *The Blackfeet-Raiders on the Northwestern Plains*. Norman, OK: University of Oklahoma Press, 1958.

———. *The Story of the Blackfeet*. Washington, D.C.: Department of the Interior, Haskell Press, 1944.

Hoover, Herbert T., ed. *A New South Dakota History*. Sioux Falls, SD: The Center for Western Studies, 2005.

Hurst, David Thomas, et al. *The Native Americans: An Illustrated History*. Atlanta, GA: Turner Publishing, Inc., 1993.

Laubin, Reginald, and Gladys Laubin. *The Indian Tipi: Its History, Construction, and Use*. Norman, OK: University of Oklahoma Press, 1957.

Neihardt, John G. *Black Elk Speaks*. 1932. Reprinted 1988 by Bison Books. Page references are to the 1988 edition, seventh printing.

Pelta, Kathy. *The Royal Roads: Spanish Trails in North America*. Austin, TX: Raintree Steck-Vaughn Publishing Company, 1997.

Standing Bear, Luther. *My People the Sioux*. 1928. Reprint, Lincoln, NE: University of Nebraska Press, 1975.

Taylor, Colin F. *The Plains Indians*. Avenel, NJ: Crescent Books, 1994.

———. *Saam*. Wyk auf Föhr, Germany: Verlag für Amerikanistik, 1993.

———. *Sun'ka Wakan*. Wyk auf Föhr, Germany: Verlag für Amerikanistik, 1995.

———. *Wapa'ha*. Wyk auf Föhr, Germany: Verlag für Amerikanistik, 1994.

———. *Yupika*. Wyk auf Föhr, Germany: Verlag für Amerikanistik, 1997.

Taylor, William O. *With Custer on the Little Bighorn*. Edited by Greg Martin. New York: Viking, 1996.

Tillet, Leslie. *Wind on the Buffalo Grass*. New York: Crowell, 1976.

Trimble, Michael K. *An Ethnohistorical Interpretation of the Spread of Smallpox in the Northern Plains Utilizing Concepts of Disease Ecology*. Lincoln, NE: J & L Reprint Company, 1986.

Ward, Geoffrey C. *The West: An Illustrated History*. New York: Little Brown and Company, 1996.

Weatherford, Jack M. *Indian Givers: How the Indians of the Americas Transformed the World*. New York: Fawcett Columbine, 1988.

Index

Page numbers in italics refer to illustrations.

The paintings for this book were created with acrylic paint on 140 lb. cold-press 100-percent-cotton acid-free paper. The drawings were made with black colored pencil on heavyweight watercolor paper.

IMAGE CREDITS

All of the paintings and line drawings in this book are by S. D. Nelson, except Red Horse's drawing on page 26. The border seen on most pages is a design based on traditional Lakota geometric patterns. The photographs and archival images are reproduced by courtesy of the following sources:

National Anthropological Archives, Smithsonian Institution: front cover, spine, and pp. 3 (NAINV00506100), 8 (left—NAINV09852600), 8 (right—NAINV09851300), 26 (NAINV008570300), 36 (NAINV06081800); Library of Congress collection: pp. 12, 24 (bottom), 33, 35, 37 (top), 37 (bottom); Nebraska Historical Society: p. 13 (top); CORBIS: p. 13 (Bettmann/Corbis), 15 (Christian Barthelmess/Corbis), 22 (Bettman/Corbis), 23, 24 (top), 33 (Bettmann/Corbis), 38 (John C.H. Grabill/Corbis); Minnesota State Historical Society: p. 28 (RG2573:3-2); Denver Public Library, Western History Collection: pp. 32 (NS-710), 40 (X-31818); Buffalo Bill Historical Center: p. 34 (P.69.1800).

Library of Congress Cataloging-in-Publication Data

Nelson, S. D.
Black Elk's vision: a Lakota story / by S. D. Nelson.
p. cm.
ISBN 978-0-8109-8399-1
1. Black Elk, 1863–1950—Juvenile literature. 2. Oglala Indians—Biography—Juvenile literature. I. Title.
E99.O3B5364 2010
978.004'9752440092—dc22
[B]
2009009392

Text and illustrations copyright © 2010 S. D. Nelson
Book design by Maria T. Middleton

Printed and bound in China
10 9 8 7 6 5 4 3 2 1

Abrams Books for Young Readers are available at special discounts when purchased in quantity for premiums and promotions as well as fundraising or educational use. Special editions can also be created to specification. For details, contact specialmarkets@abramsbooks.com or the address below.

ABRAMS
THE ART OF BOOKS SINCE 1949
115 West 18th Street
New York, NY 10011
www.abramsbooks.com

CANADA

MONTANA

BLACKFEET

IDAHO

R o c k y

Ft. McKenzie

Ft. Benton

Ft. Chardon

Missouri River

GREAT PLAINS

Yello

Ft. Manuel

CROW

SHOSHONE

M o u n t a i n s

BOZEMAN TRAIL

Bighorn River

Little Bighorn

BATTLE OF THE LITTLE BIGHORN

Powder River

Little Powder River

Crazy Horse

WYOMING

OREGON TRAIL

OREGON TRAIL

Ft. Larar